A GRATITUDE JOURNAL

This is my favorite Quote

> "Let us be grateful to the people who make us happy;
> they are the charming gardeners who make our souls blossom."
> Marcel Proust

I am thankful for

DATE:__/__/__

1.
2.
3.
4.

1.
2.
3.
4.

I am thankful for

DATE:__/__/__

I am thankful for

DATE:__/__/__

1.
2.
3.
4.

1.
2.
3.
4.

I am thankful for

DATE:__/__/__

I am thankful for

DATE:__/__/__

1. _______________
2. _______________
3. _______________
4. _______________

1. _______________
2. _______________
3. _______________
4. _______________

I am thankful for

DATE:__/__/__

I am thankful for

DATE:__/__/__

1. _______________
2. _______________
3. _______________
4. _______________

Cultivate an attitude of gratitude
What were the highlights of your week?

____
____
____
____

> "We take for granted the very things that most deserve our gratitude."
>
> Cynthia Ozick

I am thankful for

DATE:__/__/__

1. ___________________________
2. ___________________________
3. ___________________________
4. ___________________________

1. ___________________________
2. ___________________________
3. ___________________________
4. ___________________________

I am thankful for

DATE:__/__/__

I am thankful for

DATE:__/__/__

1. ___________________________
2. ___________________________
3. ___________________________
4. ___________________________

1. ___________________________
2. ___________________________
3. ___________________________
4. ___________________________

I am thankful for

DATE:__/__/__

I am thankful for

DATE:__/__/__

1.
2.
3.
4.

1.
2.
3.
4.

I am thankful for

DATE:__/__/__

I am thankful for

DATE:__/__/__

1.
2.
3.
4.

Cultivate an attitude of gratitude
What were the highlights of your week?

"Be mindful. Be grateful. Be positive. Be true. Be kind."
Roy T. Bennett, The Light in the Heart

I am thankful for

DATE:__/__/__

1. _______________________________
2. _______________________________
3. _______________________________
4. _______________________________

1. _______________________________
2. _______________________________
3. _______________________________
4. _______________________________

I am thankful for

DATE:__/__/__

I am thankful for

DATE:__/__/__

1. _______________________________
2. _______________________________
3. _______________________________
4. _______________________________

1. _______________________________
2. _______________________________
3. _______________________________
4. _______________________________

I am thankful for

DATE:__/__/__

I am thankful for

DATE:__/__/__

1. ______________________
2. ______________________
3. ______________________
4. ______________________

1. ______________________
2. ______________________
3. ______________________
4. ______________________

I am thankful for

DATE:__/__/__

I am thankful for

DATE:__/__/__

1. ______________________
2. ______________________
3. ______________________
4. ______________________

Cultivate an attitude of gratitude
What were the highlights of your week?

____
____
____
____

> "Do not spoil what you have by desiring what you have not;
> remember that what you now have was once among
> the things you only hoped for."
>
> Epicurus

I am thankful for

DATE:__/__/__

1. ______________________________
2. ______________________________
3. ______________________________
4. ______________________________

1. ______________________________
2. ______________________________
3. ______________________________
4. ______________________________

I am thankful for

DATE:__/__/__

I am thankful for

DATE:__/__/__

1. ______________________________
2. ______________________________
3. ______________________________
4. ______________________________

1. ______________________________
2. ______________________________
3. ______________________________
4. ______________________________

I am thankful for

DATE:__/__/__

I am thankful for

DATE:__/__/__

1. _______________________________
2. _______________________________
3. _______________________________
4. _______________________________

1. _______________________________
2. _______________________________
3. _______________________________
4. _______________________________

I am thankful for

DATE:__/__/__

I am thankful for

DATE:__/__/__

1. _______________________________
2. _______________________________
3. _______________________________
4. _______________________________

Cultivate an attitude of gratitude
What were the highlights of your week?

____
____
____
____

> "Be thankful for everything that happens in your life;
> it's all an experience."
> Roy T. Bennett

I am thankful for

DATE:__/__/__

1. _______________________________
2. _______________________________
3. _______________________________
4. _______________________________

1. _______________________________
2. _______________________________
3. _______________________________
4. _______________________________

I am thankful for

DATE:__/__/__

I am thankful for

DATE:__/__/__

1. _______________________________
2. _______________________________
3. _______________________________
4. _______________________________

1. _______________________________
2. _______________________________
3. _______________________________
4. _______________________________

I am thankful for

DATE:__/__/__

I am thankful for

DATE:__/__/__

1. _______________________________
2. _______________________________
3. _______________________________
4. _______________________________

1. _______________________________
2. _______________________________
3. _______________________________
4. _______________________________

I am thankful for

DATE:__/__/__

I am thankful for

DATE:__/__/__

1. _______________________________
2. _______________________________
3. _______________________________
4. _______________________________

Cultivate an attitude of gratitude
What were the highlights of your week?

____

____

____

____

> "Piglet noticed that even though he had a Very Small Heart,
> it could hold a rather large amount of Gratitude."
> A.A. Milne, Winnie-the-Pooh

I am thankful for

DATE:__/__/__

1. _______________________
2. _______________________
3. _______________________
4. _______________________

1. _______________________
2. _______________________
3. _______________________
4. _______________________

I am thankful for

DATE:__/__/__

I am thankful for

DATE:__/__/__

1. _______________________
2. _______________________
3. _______________________
4. _______________________

1. _______________________
2. _______________________
3. _______________________
4. _______________________

I am thankful for

DATE:__/__/__

I am thankful for

DATE:__/__/__

1.
2.
3.
4.

1.
2.
3.
4.

I am thankful for

DATE:__/__/__

I am thankful for

DATE:__/__/__

1.
2.
3.
4.

Cultivate an attitude of gratitude
What were the highlights of your week?

Great things happen to those who don't stop believing,
trying, learning, and being grateful."
Roy T. Bennett, The Light in the Heart

I am thankful for

DATE:__/__/__

1. _______________________________
2. _______________________________
3. _______________________________
4. _______________________________

1. _______________________________
2. _______________________________
3. _______________________________
4. _______________________________

I am thankful for

DATE:__/__/__

I am thankful for

DATE:__/__/__

1. _______________________________
2. _______________________________
3. _______________________________
4. _______________________________

1. _______________________________
2. _______________________________
3. _______________________________
4. _______________________________

I am thankful for

DATE:__/__/__

I am thankful for
DATE:__/__/__

1.
2.
3.
4.

1.
2.
3.
4.

I am thankful for
DATE:__/__/__

I am thankful for
DATE:__/__/__

1.
2.
3.
4.

Cultivate an attitude of gratitude
What were the highlights of your week?

"Let us be grateful to the people who make us happy;
they are the charming gardeners who make our souls blossom."
Marcel Proust

I am thankful for

DATE:__/__/__

1. ___________________________________
2. ___________________________________
3. ___________________________________
4. ___________________________________

1. ___________________________________
2. ___________________________________
3. ___________________________________
4. ___________________________________

I am thankful for

DATE:__/__/__

I am thankful for

DATE:__/__/__

1. ___________________________________
2. ___________________________________
3. ___________________________________
4. ___________________________________

1. ___________________________________
2. ___________________________________
3. ___________________________________
4. ___________________________________

I am thankful for

DATE:__/__/__

I am thankful for

DATE:__/__/__

1.
2.
3.
4.

1.
2.
3.
4.

I am thankful for

DATE:__/__/__

I am thankful for

DATE:__/__/__

1.
2.
3.
4.

Cultivate an attitude of gratitude
What were the highlights of your week?

> "I would maintain that thanks are the highest form of thought;
> and that gratitude is happiness doubled by wonder."
> G.K. Chesterton

I am thankful for

DATE:__/__/__

1. ___________________________
2. ___________________________
3. ___________________________
4. ___________________________

1. ___________________________
2. ___________________________
3. ___________________________
4. ___________________________

I am thankful for

DATE:__/__/__

I am thankful for

DATE:__/__/__

1. ___________________________
2. ___________________________
3. ___________________________
4. ___________________________

1. ___________________________
2. ___________________________
3. ___________________________
4. ___________________________

I am thankful for

DATE:__/__/__

I am thankful for

DATE:__/__/__

1. _______________________
2. _______________________
3. _______________________
4. _______________________

1. _______________________
2. _______________________
3. _______________________
4. _______________________

I am thankful for

DATE:__/__/__

I am thankful for

DATE:__/__/__

1. _______________________
2. _______________________
3. _______________________
4. _______________________

Cultivate an attitude of gratitude
What were the highlights of your week?

____
____
____
____

"If the only prayer you said was thank you,
that would be enough."
Meister Eckhart

I am thankful for

DATE:__/__/__

1. _______________________________________
2. _______________________________________
3. _______________________________________
4. _______________________________________

1. _______________________________________
2. _______________________________________
3. _______________________________________
4. _______________________________________

I am thankful for

DATE:__/__/__

I am thankful for

DATE:__/__/__

1. _______________________________________
2. _______________________________________
3. _______________________________________
4. _______________________________________

1. _______________________________________
2. _______________________________________
3. _______________________________________
4. _______________________________________

I am thankful for

DATE:__/__/__

I am thankful for

DATE:__/__/__

1. _______________________________
2. _______________________________
3. _______________________________
4. _______________________________

1. _______________________________
2. _______________________________
3. _______________________________
4. _______________________________

I am thankful for

DATE:__/__/__

I am thankful for

DATE:__/__/__

1. _______________________________
2. _______________________________
3. _______________________________
4. _______________________________

Cultivate an attitude of gratitude
What were the highlights of your week?

____
____
____
____

> "When we give cheerfully and accept gratefully,
> everyone is blessed."
> Maya Angelou

I am thankful for

DATE: __/__/__

1. ____
2. ____
3. ____
4. ____

1. ____
2. ____
3. ____
4. ____

I am thankful for

DATE: __/__/__

I am thankful for

DATE: __/__/__

1. ____
2. ____
3. ____
4. ____

1. ____
2. ____
3. ____
4. ____

I am thankful for

DATE: __/__/__

I am thankful for

DATE:__/__/__

1.
2.
3.
4.

1.
2.
3.
4.

I am thankful for

DATE:__/__/__

I am thankful for

DATE:__/__/__

1.
2.
3.
4.

Cultivate an attitude of gratitude
What were the highlights of your week?

"We must find time to stop and thank
the people who make a difference in our lives."
John F. Kennedy

I am thankful for

DATE:__/__/__

1. ___________________________
2. ___________________________
3. ___________________________
4. ___________________________

1. ___________________________
2. ___________________________
3. ___________________________
4. ___________________________

I am thankful for

DATE:__/__/__

I am thankful for

DATE:__/__/__

1. ___________________________
2. ___________________________
3. ___________________________
4. ___________________________

1. ___________________________
2. ___________________________
3. ___________________________
4. ___________________________

I am thankful for

DATE:__/__/__

I am thankful for

DATE:__/__/__

1. ________________________________
2. ________________________________
3. ________________________________
4. ________________________________

1. ________________________________
2. ________________________________
3. ________________________________
4. ________________________________

I am thankful for

DATE:__/__/__

I am thankful for

DATE:__/__/__

1. ________________________________
2. ________________________________
3. ________________________________
4. ________________________________

Cultivate an attitude of gratitude
What were the highlights of your week?

____
____
____
____

> "If having a soul means being able to feel love and loyalty
> and gratitude, then animals are better
> off than a lot of humans."
> James Herriot , All Creatures Great and Small

I am thankful for

DATE:__/__/__

1. __________________________
2. __________________________
3. __________________________
4. __________________________

1. __________________________
2. __________________________
3. __________________________
4. __________________________

I am thankful for

DATE:__/__/__

I am thankful for

DATE:__/__/__

1. __________________________
2. __________________________
3. __________________________
4. __________________________

1. __________________________
2. __________________________
3. __________________________
4. __________________________

I am thankful for

DATE:__/__/__

_______________________ 1. _________________________________

I am thankful for 2. _________________________________

DATE:__/__/__ 3. _________________________________

_______________________ 4. _________________________________

1. _________________________________

2. _________________________________ _______________________

3. _________________________________ I am thankful for

4. _________________________________ DATE:__/__/__

____

_______________________ 1. _________________________________

I am thankful for 2. _________________________________

DATE:__/__/__ 3. _________________________________

_______________________ 4. _________________________________

Cultivate an attitude of gratitude
What were the highlights of your week?

____

____

____

____

> "When one has a grateful heart, life is so beautiful."
> Roy T. Bennett, The Light in the Heart

I am thankful for

DATE:__/__/__

1.
2.
3.
4.

1.
2.
3.
4.

I am thankful for

DATE:__/__/__

I am thankful for

DATE:__/__/__

1.
2.
3.
4.

1.
2.
3.
4.

I am thankful for

DATE:__/__/__

I am thankful for

DATE:__/__/__

1.

2.

3.

4.

1.

2.

3.

4.

I am thankful for

DATE:__/__/__

I am thankful for

DATE:__/__/__

1.

2.

3.

4.

Cultivate an attitude of gratitude
What were the highlights of your week?

> "Showing gratitude is one of the simplest yet most powerful
> things humans can do for each other."
> Randy Pausch, The Last Lecture

I am thankful for

DATE:__/__/__

1.
2.
3.
4.

1.
2.
3.
4.

I am thankful for

DATE:__/__/__

I am thankful for

DATE:__/__/__

1.
2.
3.
4.

1.
2.
3.
4.

I am thankful for

DATE:__/__/__

I am thankful for

DATE:__/__/__

1.

2.

3.

4.

1.

2.

3.

4.

I am thankful for

DATE:__/__/__

I am thankful for

DATE:__/__/__

1.

2.

3.

4.

Cultivate an attitude of gratitude
What were the highlights of your week?

"Gratitude is not only the greatest of virtues,
but the parent of all others."
Marcus Tullius Cicero

I am thankful for

DATE:__/__/__

1.
2.
3.
4.

1.
2.
3.
4.

I am thankful for

DATE:__/__/__

I am thankful for

DATE:__/__/__

1.
2.
3.
4.

1.
2.
3.
4.

I am thankful for

DATE:__/__/__

I am thankful for

DATE:__/__/__

1. _______________________________
2. _______________________________
3. _______________________________
4. _______________________________

1. _______________________________
2. _______________________________
3. _______________________________
4. _______________________________

I am thankful for

DATE:__/__/__

I am thankful for

DATE:__/__/__

1. _______________________________
2. _______________________________
3. _______________________________
4. _______________________________

Cultivate an attitude of gratitude
What were the highlights of your week?

____
____
____
____

> "Appreciation is a wonderful thing.
> It makes what is excellent in others belong to us as well."
> Voltaire

I am thankful for

DATE:__/__/__

1. __________________________________
2. __________________________________
3. __________________________________
4. __________________________________

1. __________________________________
2. __________________________________
3. __________________________________
4. __________________________________

I am thankful for

DATE:__/__/__

I am thankful for

DATE:__/__/__

1. __________________________________
2. __________________________________
3. __________________________________
4. __________________________________

1. __________________________________
2. __________________________________
3. __________________________________
4. __________________________________

I am thankful for

DATE:__/__/__

I am thankful for

DATE:__/__/__

1. _______________________________
2. _______________________________
3. _______________________________
4. _______________________________

1. _______________________________
2. _______________________________
3. _______________________________
4. _______________________________

I am thankful for

DATE:__/__/__

I am thankful for

DATE:__/__/__

1. _______________________________
2. _______________________________
3. _______________________________
4. _______________________________

Cultivate an attitude of gratitude
What were the highlights of your week?

____
____
____
____

> "...for love casts out fear, and gratitude can conquer pride."
> Louisa May Alcott, Little Women

I am thankful for

DATE:__/__/__

1. ____
2. ____
3. ____
4. ____

1. ____
2. ____
3. ____
4. ____

I am thankful for

DATE:__/__/__

I am thankful for

DATE:__/__/__

1. ____
2. ____
3. ____
4. ____

1. ____
2. ____
3. ____
4. ____

I am thankful for

DATE:__/__/__

I am thankful for

DATE:__/__/__

1. ____________________
2. ____________________
3. ____________________
4. ____________________

1. ____________________
2. ____________________
3. ____________________
4. ____________________

I am thankful for

DATE:__/__/__

I am thankful for

DATE:__/__/__

1. ____________________
2. ____________________
3. ____________________
4. ____________________

Cultivate an attitude of gratitude
What were the highlights of your week?

____
____
____
____

> "As we express our gratitude, we must never forget that
> the highest appreciation is not to utter words,
> but to live by them.
> John F. Kennedy

I am thankful for

DATE:__/__/__

1.
2.
3.
4.

1.
2.
3.
4.

I am thankful for

DATE:__/__/__

I am thankful for

DATE:__/__/__

1.
2.
3.
4.

1.
2.
3.
4.

I am thankful for

DATE:__/__/__

I am thankful for

DATE:__/__/__

1. _______________________
2. _______________________
3. _______________________
4. _______________________

1. _______________________
2. _______________________
3. _______________________
4. _______________________

I am thankful for

DATE:__/__/__

I am thankful for

DATE:__/__/__

1. _______________________
2. _______________________
3. _______________________
4. _______________________

Cultivate an attitude of gratitude
What were the highlights of your week?

____
____
____
____

> "Gratitude looks to the Past and love to the Present;
> fear, avarice, lust, and ambition look ahead."
> C.S. Lewis, The Screwtape Letters

I am thankful for

DATE:__/__/__

1. ____
2. ____
3. ____
4. ____

1. ____
2. ____
3. ____
4. ____

I am thankful for

DATE:__/__/__

I am thankful for

DATE:__/__/__

1. ____
2. ____
3. ____
4. ____

1. ____
2. ____
3. ____
4. ____

I am thankful for

DATE:__/__/__

I am thankful for

DATE:__/__/__

1.
2.
3.
4.

1.
2.
3.
4.

I am thankful for

DATE:__/__/__

I am thankful for

DATE:__/__/__

1.
2.
3.
4.

Cultivate an attitude of gratitude
What were the highlights of your week?

I am thankful for

DATE:__/__/__

1.
2.
3.
4.

1.
2.
3.
4.

I am thankful for

DATE:__/__/__

I am thankful for

DATE:__/__/__

1.
2.
3.
4.

1.
2.
3.
4.

I am thankful for

DATE:__/__/__

I am thankful for

DATE:__/__/__

1.
2.
3.
4.

1.
2.
3.
4.

I am thankful for

DATE:__/__/__

I am thankful for

DATE:__/__/__

1.
2.
3.
4.

Cultivate an attitude of gratitude
What were the highlights of your week?

> "When you are grateful, fear disappears and abundance appears."
> Anthony Robbins

I am thankful for

DATE:__/__/__

1. _______________________________
2. _______________________________
3. _______________________________
4. _______________________________

1. _______________________________
2. _______________________________
3. _______________________________
4. _______________________________

I am thankful for

DATE:__/__/__

I am thankful for

DATE:__/__/__

1. _______________________________
2. _______________________________
3. _______________________________
4. _______________________________

1. _______________________________
2. _______________________________
3. _______________________________
4. _______________________________

I am thankful for

DATE:__/__/__

I am thankful for

DATE:__/__/__

1.

2.

3.

4.

1.

2.

3.

4.

I am thankful for

DATE:__/__/__

I am thankful for

DATE:__/__/__

1.

2.

3.

4.

Cultivate an attitude of gratitude
What were the highlights of your week?

> "We should certainly count our blessings,
> but we should also make our blessings count."
> Neal A. Maxwell

I am thankful for

DATE:__/__/__

1. _______________________________
2. _______________________________
3. _______________________________
4. _______________________________

1. _______________________________
2. _______________________________
3. _______________________________
4. _______________________________

I am thankful for

DATE:__/__/__

I am thankful for

DATE:__/__/__

1. _______________________________
2. _______________________________
3. _______________________________
4. _______________________________

1. _______________________________
2. _______________________________
3. _______________________________
4. _______________________________

I am thankful for

DATE:__/__/__

I am thankful for

DATE:__/__/__

1. ____________________________
2. ____________________________
3. ____________________________
4. ____________________________

1. ____________________________
2. ____________________________
3. ____________________________
4. ____________________________

I am thankful for

DATE:__/__/__

I am thankful for

DATE:__/__/__

1. ____________________________
2. ____________________________
3. ____________________________
4. ____________________________

Cultivate an attitude of gratitude
What were the highlights of your week?

____
____
____
____

I am thankful for

DATE:__/__/__

1.
2.
3.
4.

1.
2.
3.
4.

I am thankful for

DATE:__/__/__

I am thankful for

DATE:__/__/__

1.
2.
3.
4.

1.
2.
3.
4.

I am thankful for

DATE:__/__/__

I am thankful for

DATE:__/__/__

1. __________________________
2. __________________________
3. __________________________
4. __________________________

1. __________________________
2. __________________________
3. __________________________
4. __________________________

I am thankful for

DATE:__/__/__

I am thankful for

DATE:__/__/__

1. __________________________
2. __________________________
3. __________________________
4. __________________________

Cultivate an attitude of gratitude
What were the highlights of your week?

____
____
____
____

> "Be happy with who you are and what you do,
> and you can do anything you want."
> Steve Maraboli, Life, the Truth, and Being Free

I am thankful for

DATE:__/__/__

1. ___________________________
2. ___________________________
3. ___________________________
4. ___________________________

1. ___________________________
2. ___________________________
3. ___________________________
4. ___________________________

I am thankful for

DATE:__/__/__

I am thankful for

DATE:__/__/__

1. ___________________________
2. ___________________________
3. ___________________________
4. ___________________________

1. ___________________________
2. ___________________________
3. ___________________________
4. ___________________________

I am thankful for

DATE:__/__/__

I am thankful for

DATE:__/__/__

1. __________________________________
2. __________________________________
3. __________________________________
4. __________________________________

1. __________________________________
2. __________________________________
3. __________________________________
4. __________________________________

I am thankful for

DATE:__/__/__

I am thankful for

DATE:__/__/__

1. __________________________________
2. __________________________________
3. __________________________________
4. __________________________________

Cultivate an attitude of gratitude
What were the highlights of your week?

____
____
____
____

> "God gave you a gift of 86,400 seconds today.
> Have you used one to say thank you "
> William Arthur Ward

I am thankful for

DATE:__/__/__

1. _______________________________
2. _______________________________
3. _______________________________
4. _______________________________

1. _______________________________
2. _______________________________
3. _______________________________
4. _______________________________

I am thankful for

DATE:__/__/__

I am thankful for

DATE:__/__/__

1. _______________________________
2. _______________________________
3. _______________________________
4. _______________________________

1. _______________________________
2. _______________________________
3. _______________________________
4. _______________________________

I am thankful for

DATE:__/__/__

I am thankful for

DATE:__/__/__

1. ____________________________________
2. ____________________________________
3. ____________________________________
4. ____________________________________

1. ____________________________________
2. ____________________________________
3. ____________________________________
4. ____________________________________

I am thankful for

DATE:__/__/__

I am thankful for

DATE:__/__/__

1. ____________________________________
2. ____________________________________
3. ____________________________________
4. ____________________________________

Cultivate an attitude of gratitude
What were the highlights of your week?

____

____

____

____

> "What separates privilege from entitlement is gratitude."
> Brené Brown

I am thankful for

DATE:__/__/__

1.
2.
3.
4.

1.
2.
3.
4.

I am thankful for

DATE:__/__/__

I am thankful for

DATE:__/__/__

1.
2.
3.
4.

1.
2.
3.
4.

I am thankful for

DATE:__/__/__

I am thankful for

DATE:__/__/__

1.

2.

3.

4.

1.

2.

3.

4.

I am thankful for

DATE:__/__/__

I am thankful for

DATE:__/__/__

1.

2.

3.

4.

Cultivate an attitude of gratitude
What were the highlights of your week?

"Keeping your body healthy is an expression of gratitude
to the whole cosmos - the trees, the clouds, everything."
Thich Nhat Hanh

I am thankful for

DATE:__/__/__

1.
2.
3.
4.

1.
2.
3.
4.

I am thankful for

DATE:__/__/__

I am thankful for

DATE:__/__/__

1.
2.
3.
4.

1.
2.
3.
4.

I am thankful for

DATE:__/__/__

I am thankful for

DATE:__/__/__

1.
2.
3.
4.

1.
2.
3.
4.

I am thankful for

DATE:__/__/__

I am thankful for

DATE:__/__/__

1.
2.
3.
4.

Cultivate an attitude of gratitude
What were the highlights of your week?

"Feeling gratitude and not expressing it is like
wrapping a present and not giving it."
William Arthur Ward

I am thankful for

DATE:__/__/__

1.
2.
3.
4.

1.
2.
3.
4.

I am thankful for

DATE:__/__/__

I am thankful for

DATE:__/__/__

1.
2.
3.
4.

1.
2.
3.
4.

I am thankful for

DATE:__/__/__

I am thankful for

DATE:__/__/__

1.
2.
3.
4.

1.
2.
3.
4.

I am thankful for

DATE:__/__/__

I am thankful for

DATE:__/__/__

1.
2.
3.
4.

Cultivate an attitude of gratitude
What were the highlights of your week?

> "Those who have the ability to be grateful are the ones
> who have the ability to achieve greatness."
> Steve Maraboli, Life, the Truth, and Being Free

I am thankful for

DATE:__/__/__

1. ______________________________
2. ______________________________
3. ______________________________
4. ______________________________

1. ______________________________
2. ______________________________
3. ______________________________
4. ______________________________

I am thankful for

DATE:__/__/__

I am thankful for

DATE:__/__/__

1. ______________________________
2. ______________________________
3. ______________________________
4. ______________________________

1. ______________________________
2. ______________________________
3. ______________________________
4. ______________________________

I am thankful for

DATE:__/__/__

I am thankful for

DATE:__/__/__

1.
2.
3.
4.

1.
2.
3.
4.

I am thankful for

DATE:__/__/__

I am thankful for

DATE:__/__/__

1.
2.
3.
4.

Cultivate an attitude of gratitude
What were the highlights of your week?

> "Got no checkbooks, got no banks.
> Still I'd like to express my thanks
> I've got the sun in the mornin' and the moon at night."
> Irving Berlin

I am thankful for

DATE:__/__/__

1. _______________________________
2. _______________________________
3. _______________________________
4. _______________________________

1. _______________________________
2. _______________________________
3. _______________________________
4. _______________________________

I am thankful for

DATE:__/__/__

I am thankful for

DATE:__/__/__

1. _______________________________
2. _______________________________
3. _______________________________
4. _______________________________

1. _______________________________
2. _______________________________
3. _______________________________
4. _______________________________

I am thankful for

DATE:__/__/__

I am thankful for

DATE:__/__/__

1. __________________________
2. __________________________
3. __________________________
4. __________________________

1. __________________________
2. __________________________
3. __________________________
4. __________________________

I am thankful for

DATE:__/__/__

I am thankful for

DATE:__/__/__

1. __________________________
2. __________________________
3. __________________________
4. __________________________

Cultivate an attitude of gratitude
What were the highlights of your week?

____
____
____
____

> "Happiness can only be achieved by looking inward & learning
> to enjoy whatever life has and this requires
> transforming greed into gratitude."
> John Chrysostom

I am thankful for

DATE:__/__/__

1. _______________________
2. _______________________
3. _______________________
4. _______________________

1. _______________________
2. _______________________
3. _______________________
4. _______________________

I am thankful for

DATE:__/__/__

I am thankful for

DATE:__/__/__

1. _______________________
2. _______________________
3. _______________________
4. _______________________

1. _______________________
2. _______________________
3. _______________________
4. _______________________

I am thankful for

DATE:__/__/__

I am thankful for

DATE:__/__/__

1. _______________________
2. _______________________
3. _______________________
4. _______________________

1. _______________________
2. _______________________
3. _______________________
4. _______________________

I am thankful for

DATE:__/__/__

I am thankful for

DATE:__/__/__

1. _______________________
2. _______________________
3. _______________________
4. _______________________

Cultivate an attitude of gratitude
What were the highlights of your week?

____
____
____
____

"In ordinary life we hardly realize that we receive a great deal more than we give, and that it is only with gratitude that life becomes rich."
Deitrich Bonhoeffer

I am thankful for

DATE:__/__/__

1.
2.
3.
4.

1.
2.
3.
4.

I am thankful for

DATE:__/__/__

I am thankful for

DATE:__/__/__

1.
2.
3.
4.

1.
2.
3.
4.

I am thankful for

DATE:__/__/__

I am thankful for

DATE:__/__/__

1. _______________________________
2. _______________________________
3. _______________________________
4. _______________________________

1. _______________________________
2. _______________________________
3. _______________________________
4. _______________________________

I am thankful for

DATE:__/__/__

I am thankful for

DATE:__/__/__

1. _______________________________
2. _______________________________
3. _______________________________
4. _______________________________

Cultivate an attitude of gratitude
What were the highlights of your week?

____
____
____
____

"At times our own light goes out and is rekindled by a spark from another person. Each of us has cause to think with deep gratitude of those who have lighted the flame within us."
Albert Schweitzer

I am thankful for

DATE:__/__/__

1. ___________________________________
2. ___________________________________
3. ___________________________________
4. ___________________________________

1. ___________________________________
2. ___________________________________
3. ___________________________________
4. ___________________________________

I am thankful for

DATE:__/__/__

I am thankful for

DATE:__/__/__

1. ___________________________________
2. ___________________________________
3. ___________________________________
4. ___________________________________

1. ___________________________________
2. ___________________________________
3. ___________________________________
4. ___________________________________

I am thankful for

DATE:__/__/__

I am thankful for

DATE:___/___/__

1. _______________________________
2. _______________________________
3. _______________________________
4. _______________________________

1. _______________________________
2. _______________________________
3. _______________________________
4. _______________________________

I am thankful for

DATE:___/___/__

I am thankful for

DATE:___/___/__

1. _______________________________
2. _______________________________
3. _______________________________
4. _______________________________

Cultivate an attitude of gratitude
What were the highlights of your week?

____
____
____
____

"It's a funny thing about life, once you begin to take note
of the things you are grateful for, you begin to
lose sight of the things that you lack."
Germany Kent

I am thankful for

DATE:__/__/__

1. _______________________________________
2. _______________________________________
3. _______________________________________
4. _______________________________________

1. _______________________________________
2. _______________________________________
3. _______________________________________
4. _______________________________________

I am thankful for

DATE:__/__/__

I am thankful for

DATE:__/__/__

1. _______________________________________
2. _______________________________________
3. _______________________________________
4. _______________________________________

1. _______________________________________
2. _______________________________________
3. _______________________________________
4. _______________________________________

I am thankful for

DATE:__/__/__

I am thankful for

DATE:__/__/__

1. _______________________________
2. _______________________________
3. _______________________________
4. _______________________________

1. _______________________________
2. _______________________________
3. _______________________________
4. _______________________________

I am thankful for

DATE:__/__/__

I am thankful for

DATE:__/__/__

1. _______________________________
2. _______________________________
3. _______________________________
4. _______________________________

Cultivate an attitude of gratitude
What were the highlights of your week?

____
____
____
____

An attitude of gratitude brings great things."
Yogi Bhajan

I am thankful for

DATE:__/__/__

1.
2.
3.
4.

1.
2.
3.
4.

I am thankful for

DATE:__/__/__

I am thankful for

DATE:__/__/__

1.
2.
3.
4.

1.
2.
3.
4.

I am thankful for

DATE:__/__/__

I am thankful for

DATE:__/__/__

1. _______________________________
2. _______________________________
3. _______________________________
4. _______________________________

1. _______________________________
2. _______________________________
3. _______________________________
4. _______________________________

I am thankful for

DATE:__/__/__

I am thankful for

DATE:__/__/__

1. _______________________________
2. _______________________________
3. _______________________________
4. _______________________________

Cultivate an attitude of gratitude
What were the highlights of your week?

____
____
____
____

> "There is power in having gratitude and giving thanks for what you have; it attracts more to you."
> Idowu Koyenikan

I am thankful for

DATE:__/__/__

1. ___________________________
2. ___________________________
3. ___________________________
4. ___________________________

1. ___________________________
2. ___________________________
3. ___________________________
4. ___________________________

I am thankful for

DATE:__/__/__

I am thankful for

DATE:__/__/__

1. ___________________________
2. ___________________________
3. ___________________________
4. ___________________________

1. ___________________________
2. ___________________________
3. ___________________________
4. ___________________________

I am thankful for

DATE:__/__/__

I am thankful for

DATE:__/__/__

1. ______________________________
2. ______________________________
3. ______________________________
4. ______________________________

1. ______________________________
2. ______________________________
3. ______________________________
4. ______________________________

I am thankful for

DATE:__/__/__

I am thankful for

DATE:__/__/__

1. ______________________________
2. ______________________________
3. ______________________________
4. ______________________________

Cultivate an attitude of gratitude
What were the highlights of your week?

____

____

____

____

I am thankful for

DATE:__/__/__

1. _______________________________
2. _______________________________
3. _______________________________
4. _______________________________

1. _______________________________
2. _______________________________
3. _______________________________
4. _______________________________

I am thankful for

DATE:__/__/__

I am thankful for

DATE:__/__/__

1. _______________________________
2. _______________________________
3. _______________________________
4. _______________________________

1. _______________________________
2. _______________________________
3. _______________________________
4. _______________________________

I am thankful for

DATE:__/__/__

I am thankful for

DATE:__/__/__

1. _______________________________
2. _______________________________
3. _______________________________
4. _______________________________

1. _______________________________
2. _______________________________
3. _______________________________
4. _______________________________

I am thankful for

DATE:__/__/__

I am thankful for

DATE:__/__/__

1. _______________________________
2. _______________________________
3. _______________________________
4. _______________________________

Cultivate an attitude of gratitude
What were the highlights of your week?

____
____
____
____

> "Whatever you appreciate and give thanks for
> will increase in your life."
> Sanaya Roman

I am thankful for
DATE:__/__/__

1.____________________________
2.____________________________
3.____________________________
4.____________________________

1.____________________________
2.____________________________
3.____________________________
4.____________________________

I am thankful for
DATE:__/__/__

I am thankful for
DATE:__/__/__

1.____________________________
2.____________________________
3.____________________________
4.____________________________

1.____________________________
2.____________________________
3.____________________________
4.____________________________

I am thankful for
DATE:__/__/__

I am thankful for

DATE:__/__/__

1.
2.
3.
4.

1.
2.
3.
4.

I am thankful for

DATE:__/__/__

I am thankful for

DATE:__/__/__

1.
2.
3.
4.

Cultivate an attitude of gratitude
What were the highlights of your week?

> "Breath is the finest gift of nature.
> Be grateful for this wonderful gift."
> Amit Ray

I am thankful for

DATE:__/__/__

1. _______________________________
2. _______________________________
3. _______________________________
4. _______________________________

1. _______________________________
2. _______________________________
3. _______________________________
4. _______________________________

I am thankful for

DATE:__/__/__

I am thankful for

DATE:__/__/__

1. _______________________________
2. _______________________________
3. _______________________________
4. _______________________________

1. _______________________________
2. _______________________________
3. _______________________________
4. _______________________________

I am thankful for

DATE:__/__/__

I am thankful for

DATE:__/__/__

1.

2.

3.

4.

1.

2.

3.

4.

I am thankful for

DATE:__/__/__

I am thankful for

DATE:__/__/__

1.

2.

3.

4.

Cultivate an attitude of gratitude
What were the highlights of your week?

> "Thankfulness creates gratitude
> which generates contentment that causes peace."
> Todd Stocker

I am thankful for

DATE:__/__/__

1. _______________________________
2. _______________________________
3. _______________________________
4. _______________________________

1. _______________________________
2. _______________________________
3. _______________________________
4. _______________________________

I am thankful for

DATE:__/__/__

I am thankful for

DATE:__/__/__

1. _______________________________
2. _______________________________
3. _______________________________
4. _______________________________

1. _______________________________
2. _______________________________
3. _______________________________
4. _______________________________

I am thankful for

DATE:__/__/__

I am thankful for

DATE:__/__/__

1. ___________________
2. ___________________
3. ___________________
4. ___________________

1. ___________________
2. ___________________
3. ___________________
4. ___________________

I am thankful for

DATE:__/__/__

I am thankful for

DATE:__/__/__

1. ___________________
2. ___________________
3. ___________________
4. ___________________

Cultivate an attitude of gratitude
What were the highlights of your week?

____
____
____
____

> "There is strange comfort in knowing that
> no matter what happens today, the Sun will rise again tomorrow."
> Aaron Lauritsen

I am thankful for

DATE:__/__/__

1. ____
2. ____
3. ____
4. ____

1. ____
2. ____
3. ____
4. ____

I am thankful for

DATE:__/__/__

I am thankful for

DATE:__/__/__

1. ____
2. ____
3. ____
4. ____

1. ____
2. ____
3. ____
4. ____

I am thankful for

DATE:__/__/__

I am thankful for

DATE:__/__/__

1. _______________________________________
2. _______________________________________
3. _______________________________________
4. _______________________________________

1. _______________________________________
2. _______________________________________
3. _______________________________________
4. _______________________________________

I am thankful for

DATE:__/__/__

I am thankful for

DATE:__/__/__

1. _______________________________________
2. _______________________________________
3. _______________________________________
4. _______________________________________

Cultivate an attitude of gratitude
What were the highlights of your week?

____

____

____

____

> "The essence of all beautiful art, all great art,
> is gratitude. "
> Friedrich Nietzsche

I am thankful for

DATE:__/__/__

1. _______________________________
2. _______________________________
3. _______________________________
4. _______________________________

1. _______________________________
2. _______________________________
3. _______________________________
4. _______________________________

I am thankful for

DATE:__/__/__

I am thankful for

DATE:__/__/__

1. _______________________________
2. _______________________________
3. _______________________________
4. _______________________________

1. _______________________________
2. _______________________________
3. _______________________________
4. _______________________________

I am thankful for

DATE:__/__/__

I am thankful for

DATE:__/__/__

1. ______________________________
2. ______________________________
3. ______________________________
4. ______________________________

1. ______________________________
2. ______________________________
3. ______________________________
4. ______________________________

I am thankful for

DATE:__/__/__

I am thankful for

DATE:__/__/__

1. ______________________________
2. ______________________________
3. ______________________________
4. ______________________________

Cultivate an attitude of gratitude
What were the highlights of your week?

____
____
____
____

> "The way to move out of judgement is to move into gratitude"
> Neale Donald Walsh

I am thankful for
DATE:__/__/__

1. _______________________________
2. _______________________________
3. _______________________________
4. _______________________________

1. _______________________________
2. _______________________________
3. _______________________________
4. _______________________________

I am thankful for
DATE:__/__/__

I am thankful for
DATE:__/__/__

1. _______________________________
2. _______________________________
3. _______________________________
4. _______________________________

1. _______________________________
2. _______________________________
3. _______________________________
4. _______________________________

I am thankful for
DATE:__/__/__

I am thankful for

DATE:__/__/__

1. _______________
2. _______________
3. _______________
4. _______________

1. _______________
2. _______________
3. _______________
4. _______________

I am thankful for

DATE:__/__/__

I am thankful for

DATE:__/__/__

1. _______________
2. _______________
3. _______________
4. _______________

Cultivate an attitude of gratitude
What were the highlights of your week?

____
____
____
____

"If you want to find happiness, find gratitude."
Steve Maraboli

I am thankful for

DATE:__/__/__

1. ______________________________
2. ______________________________
3. ______________________________
4. ______________________________

1. ______________________________
2. ______________________________
3. ______________________________
4. ______________________________

I am thankful for

DATE:__/__/__

I am thankful for

DATE:__/__/__

1. ______________________________
2. ______________________________
3. ______________________________
4. ______________________________

1. ______________________________
2. ______________________________
3. ______________________________
4. ______________________________

I am thankful for

DATE:__/__/__

I am thankful for

DATE:__/__/__

1.
2.
3.
4.

1.
2.
3.
4.

I am thankful for

DATE:__/__/__

I am thankful for

DATE:__/__/__

1.
2.
3.
4.

Cultivate an attitude of gratitude
What were the highlights of your week?

> "I may not be where I want to be but
> I'm thankful for not being where I used to be."
> Habeeb Akande

I am thankful for

DATE:__/__/__

1. ______________________________
2. ______________________________
3. ______________________________
4. ______________________________

1. ______________________________
2. ______________________________
3. ______________________________
4. ______________________________

I am thankful for

DATE:__/__/__

I am thankful for

DATE:__/__/__

1. ______________________________
2. ______________________________
3. ______________________________
4. ______________________________

1. ______________________________
2. ______________________________
3. ______________________________
4. ______________________________

I am thankful for

DATE:__/__/__

I am thankful for

DATE:__/__/__

1.
2.
3.
4.

1.
2.
3.
4.

I am thankful for

DATE:__/__/__

I am thankful for

DATE:__/__/__

1.
2.
3.
4.

Cultivate an attitude of gratitude
What were the highlights of your week?

"Gratitude is medicine for a heart devastated by tragedy.
If you can only be thankful for the blue sky, then do so."
richelle e. goodrich, Smile Anyway

I am thankful for

DATE:__/__/__

1. ____________________
2. ____________________
3. ____________________
4. ____________________

1. ____________________
2. ____________________
3. ____________________
4. ____________________

I am thankful for

DATE:__/__/__

I am thankful for

DATE:__/__/__

1. ____________________
2. ____________________
3. ____________________
4. ____________________

1. ____________________
2. ____________________
3. ____________________
4. ____________________

I am thankful for

DATE:__/__/__

I am thankful for

DATE:__/__/__

1.

2.

3.

4.

1.

2.

3.

4.

I am thankful for

DATE:__/__/__

I am thankful for

DATE:__/__/__

1.

2.

3.

4.

Cultivate an attitude of gratitude
What were the highlights of your week?

> "Gratitude takes less energy than anger."
> Kristin Cashore, Fire

I am thankful for

DATE:__/__/__

1. ___________________________
2. ___________________________
3. ___________________________
4. ___________________________

1. ___________________________
2. ___________________________
3. ___________________________
4. ___________________________

I am thankful for

DATE:__/__/__

I am thankful for

DATE:__/__/__

1. ___________________________
2. ___________________________
3. ___________________________
4. ___________________________

1. ___________________________
2. ___________________________
3. ___________________________
4. ___________________________

I am thankful for

DATE:__/__/__

I am thankful for

DATE:__/__/__

1. ___________________
2. ___________________
3. ___________________
4. ___________________

1. ___________________
2. ___________________
3. ___________________
4. ___________________

I am thankful for

DATE:__/__/__

I am thankful for

DATE:__/__/__

1. ___________________
2. ___________________
3. ___________________
4. ___________________

Cultivate an attitude of gratitude
What were the highlights of your week?

____

____

____

____

"Let us be grateful to the people who make us happy;
they are the charming gardeners who make our souls blossom."
Marcel Proust

I am thankful for

DATE:__/__/__

1. _______________________________
2. _______________________________
3. _______________________________
4. _______________________________

1. _______________________________
2. _______________________________
3. _______________________________
4. _______________________________

I am thankful for

DATE:__/__/__

I am thankful for

DATE:__/__/__

1. _______________________________
2. _______________________________
3. _______________________________
4. _______________________________

1. _______________________________
2. _______________________________
3. _______________________________
4. _______________________________

I am thankful for

DATE:__/__/__

I am thankful for

DATE:__/__/__

1. ___________________________
2. ___________________________
3. ___________________________
4. ___________________________

1. ___________________________
2. ___________________________
3. ___________________________
4. ___________________________

I am thankful for

DATE:__/__/__

I am thankful for

DATE:__/__/__

1. ___________________________
2. ___________________________
3. ___________________________
4. ___________________________

Cultivate an attitude of gratitude
What were the highlights of your week?

____
____
____
____

"The most beautiful moments in life are moments when you are expressing your joy, not when you are seeking it."
Jaggi Vasudev

I am thankful for

DATE:__/__/__

1.
2.
3.
4.

1.
2.
3.
4.

I am thankful for

DATE:__/__/__

I am thankful for

DATE:__/__/__

1.
2.
3.
4.

1.
2.
3.
4.

I am thankful for

DATE:__/__/__

I am thankful for

DATE:__/__/__

1. ___________________________
2. ___________________________
3. ___________________________
4. ___________________________

1. ___________________________
2. ___________________________
3. ___________________________
4. ___________________________

I am thankful for

DATE:__/__/__

I am thankful for

DATE:__/__/__

1. ___________________________
2. ___________________________
3. ___________________________
4. ___________________________

Cultivate an attitude of gratitude
What were the highlights of your week?

____
____
____
____

> "Let us be grateful to the people who make us happy;
> they are the charming gardeners who make our souls blossom."
> Marcel Proust

I am thankful for

DATE:__/__/__

1.______________________________
2.______________________________
3.______________________________
4.______________________________

1.______________________________
2.______________________________
3.______________________________
4.______________________________

I am thankful for

DATE:__/__/__

I am thankful for

DATE:__/__/__

1.______________________________
2.______________________________
3.______________________________
4.______________________________

1.______________________________
2.______________________________
3.______________________________
4.______________________________

I am thankful for

DATE:__/__/__

I am thankful for

DATE:__/__/__

1. _________________________________
2. _________________________________
3. _________________________________
4. _________________________________

1. _________________________________
2. _________________________________
3. _________________________________
4. _________________________________

I am thankful for

DATE:__/__/__

I am thankful for

DATE:__/__/__

1. _________________________________
2. _________________________________
3. _________________________________
4. _________________________________

Cultivate an attitude of gratitude
What were the highlights of your week?

____
____
____
____

I am thankful for

DATE:__/__/__

1. ______________________________
2. ______________________________
3. ______________________________
4. ______________________________

1. ______________________________
2. ______________________________
3. ______________________________
4. ______________________________

I am thankful for

DATE:__/__/__

I am thankful for

DATE:__/__/__

1. ______________________________
2. ______________________________
3. ______________________________
4. ______________________________

1. ______________________________
2. ______________________________
3. ______________________________
4. ______________________________

I am thankful for

DATE:__/__/__

I am thankful for

DATE:__/__/__

1.
2.
3.
4.

1.
2.
3.
4.

I am thankful for

DATE:__/__/__

I am thankful for

DATE:__/__/__

1.
2.
3.
4.

Cultivate an attitude of gratitude
What were the highlights of your week?